Luckhound

Poems by Timothy Tarkelly

Kansas City   Missouri

Spartan Press
Kansas City, MO
spartanpresskc.com

Copyright © Timothy Tarkelly, 2020
First Edition1 3 5 7 9 10 8 6 4 2
ISBN: 978-1-950380-91-6
LCCN: 2020932147

Design, edits and layout: Jason Ryberg
Author photo: Jeanette Powers
All rights reserved. No part of this publication may be reproduced or transmitted in any form or by any means, electronic or mechanical, including photocopying, recording or by info retrieval system, without prior written permission from the author.

The author extends an eternity's thanks to the editors, readers, designers, and everyone else who works and volunteers at the following publications that have published some of these poems:

Vaughn Street: "Still"
Philosophical Idiot: "Smarter After Midnight," "Thirties," and "Have You Ever Seen a Sunset?"
Altcoin Magazine: "Dear Satoshi" and "I Found Love on the Blockchain"
Haunted Waters Press (From the *Depths & SPLASH*): "Writers Are Gods Here"
Work to a Calm: "An Angel" and "Baptism"
Rusty Truck: "Home"
GNU: "Green"
Rise Up Review: "First Steady Paycheck and He's Trolling"
Peculiars Magazine: "Lurasidone HCl" and "Luckhound"
Whisper and the Roar: "Elegy for Industry," "Our Mothers and the Men That Guide Them," and "Heritage: Kobiety"
Typishly: "Six Shooter Blues"
Fourth & Sycamore: "Birthday" and "Meetcute"
Detritus Online: "Listening to Skip James"
Poets and War: "Achilles"
Ariel Chart: "Why Do You Act Like That?" "In My Memory, All Things Happen in Winter," "Drinks With Old Friends," "Upon Discovering the Interrobang," and "Apologies"
Riggwelter: "Maybe We Should Talk About The Bachantes Always Being the Butt of A Joke When Really They Were Just Living Their Best Lives"
Lots of Light Literary Foundation: "Dirt Dog"

From the chapbook *Fluent in Human* by Origami Poems Project: "Adventurous," "Pretty and Nice," "Overthinking," "Nostalgia," "Rust," and "Judgmental Walls"

CONTENTS

Thirties / 1

Adventurous / 2

Fenway / 3

Judgmental Walls / 4

An Angel / 5

Luckhound / 7

Lurasidone HCl / 8

It's Like Running / 9

Drinks With Old Friends / 11

The Look You Get When You're Late For Work Because Your Therapy Session Went Over Time / 12

At the Back of the Room / 13

Vacation / 14

Nostalgia / 15

Listening to Skip James / 16

Viking / 17

Six Shooter Blues / 18

Hipster / 23

Defibrillator / 24

Bombay / 25

Molehills / 26

Meetcute / 28

Spitting / 29

Thanksgiving Break at the Brass Rail / 31

In My Memory Things Always Happen in Winter / 32

The War the Night Before / 33

Michigan Goodbye / 34

Overthinking / 35

Upon Discovering the Interrobang / 36

Apologies / 37

Georgia / 38

Maybe We Should Talk About the Bacchantes
    Always Being the Butt of a Joke When Really
    They Were Just Living Their Best Lives / 39

The Boss Is in a Mood Again / 40

Dirt Dog / 45

Achilles / 46

Everyday / 47

The Social Contract / 48

Smarter After Midnight / 50

Wheel of Fortune / 51

I Found Love on the Blockchain / 52

First Steady Paycheck and He's Trolling / 54

It's a Frequency Thing / 56

Dear Satoshi / 57

Elegy For Industry / 59

Thesis / 61

Heritage: Kobiety / 63

I Am Young / 65

COMSUBLANT / 66

The Night Eddy Got Real Excited / 68

Writers Are Gods Here / 71

The World's Loneliest Moshpit, Circa 2004 / 72

Prescribed Burns / 73

Still / 74

All Before You Ended up on My Porch / 76

Have You Ever Seen a Sunset / 77

Home / 78

Our Mothers and the Men That Guide Them / 79

Baptism / 81

Makeout Spot / 84

Rust / 85

Green / 86

Birthday / 87

Pretty and Nice / 88

Why Do You Act Like That? / 89

Grammy Awards / 90

To Samie Pfeifer, you vagabond, artist of the century, always one shoulder ahead of the rest of us.

What sin have we committed that things can't be normal?

"The True Deceiver" - Tove Jansson

Bullet holes from another love,
Another life,
That weren't yours to heal.

"Bullet holes and Band Aids" - Lynne Schmidt

THIRTIES

All this talk about worldview,
about where do you get your courage from
to get up each day, to shave once in a while.
Jesus never really had to do his thirties, though.

We all just want to know
why and who we will become,
to nail our hands to it, having carried it
for everyone to see and they sing,
It is right and just.

The whole time, he had an idea,
someone filling his jugs,
changing them from bravado to wine
and he was actually doing it,
he was actually doing it.

ADVENTUROUS

The kind of people that love erratic weather
'cause they think it's their reflection:
I am such a Tempest,
a heavy blanket of ice,
but I'll melt by noon tomorrow.

Or quake when they read Kerouac:
I am such a seed in the wind,
riding the current, landing
wherever fortune will have me,
Then, off I go again.

People only say these things
at the lamest parties,
ones they've obviously been to
before, holding a beer that
doesn't taste too much like beer,
wearing a shirt that says *Bahamas*
Carnival Cruise 2002.

FENWAY

Everyone claps for Brandon, 'cause he really stepped up when the time came. Put on overalls, didn't touch anything harder than beer, only cheated once, and Mary doesn't even know about it. I guess by comparison, this is success. A seventh-inning comeback, deserving of a fan fare: an entire network of family and friends all sighing with relief. For the kid.

What it must feel like to have only put half your ass on the field, and only after a long season in the dugout. Not because you were never called to the plate, but because you were busy, dumping everyone's Gatorade on yourself, rolling in the mess. Wanting the trophy without getting off your couch.

They say angels cheer louder when the lost come home than they do for those who never stray. This is hard to hear from the pitcher's mound.

JUDGMENTAL WALLS

Tempranillo, sour-lipped
a song resting on my tongue,
but it just can't find the
air. I want to sing perfect

Spanish, but I've only had the app
for two weeks and no bards
ever found favor with *Yo
quiero una hamburguesa.*

So I talk, bouncing my wine-
soaked voice off the judgmental
walls of my apartment and shiver
at how thin it sounds.

I puff my chest like Lord Byron
And I say things Lord Byron would say,
keeping my eyes averted
from the mirror.

AN ANGEL

Gina was a bitten lip,
swollen from brute imprecision.
But even when I spat red,
I couldn't stop biting,
teasing it with my canines.
I knew better,

and so did she, but there's no arguing
not when a night seemed so endless,
awkwardly pressed between her
and a brick wall, my hands claiming
territory in spite of myself, that dumb
shit I said, my acne.
And she kissed me often.

I was blessed. She taught
me about alleyways, about
how cops are cowards
on this side of town.
Belligerence is bliss,
she would have said
if she weren't busy chugging
and puking like an angel,
in one glamorous, life-giving spew
like Moses' rock in the desert.

A golden calf, brilliant
in the sun, with so many mouths
chanting for it.
I was one of them, fevered,
praying for the chance,
to rub my fingers along the trim.

The others built her up
just to point, touch and call
her sinful, a slut. She fell,
and always fell so hard,
turning rounded corners
into pikes. Soft edges drowned
out by that famed belligerence.

I thought I had arms
built to catch such a cosmic force.
I know she wasn't a slut, 'cause
that's not a real thing. 'Cause
she told me so. 'Cause
she cried when she overheard it,
when men left her to smolder
and reignite her own embers
with booze and repetition.

They called her a lot of things,
but she just did what she wanted,
what she had to.
Gina taught me so much.

LUCKHOUND

Guilt has me
squinting at scratch-card math.
Throwing mud over my shoulder
'cause it's heavier than salt.
Squeezing the living, kicking rabbit
to get my lips at its feet.
Blowing kisses and wishes
to rubber-molded martyrs
and rubbing painted bellies
of sawed trunks, turned to idols.
Softer slurps of goat horn soup
still burn my tongue (penance
for mocking an ancient, island religion).
Hearing the strained, dead-air wheeze of my wallet,
emaciated and poked
by every passing screen —
those windows to helpful heaven.
Swiping left for a whole new chapter
to be afraid of,
a whole new convoy
of junk to dampen the rumble,
and a whole new crop
of growing prices.

LURASIDONE HCL

Goodbye heart, I'll miss you.
I already see the outline, a blown-out wall;
a self-shaped hole in the wood.
You'd rather leap than chat. I'll miss
your voice the most, the way it calms
me, even when you say scary shit
about switchblades, old phone numbers.
Even horror glows a little
with a voice like that,
all passion and alveolar trills.
You sound like Gabo.
Say noradrenaline again.

I'd promise to write, but who knows
who I'll be in two weeks. When, where
things will happen, if clocks will still work
for me. Maybe, I've been seeing numbers
differently than I'm supposed to. I've read
this is normal. Do people write letters
when they're happy? Good thing
they make forever stamps.
Somebody will use them someday.

IT'S LIKE RUNNING

I often wonder if I read poems too fast.
Am I breathing at the right spot,
respecting the pregnant comma
the way Mrs. Rehmert taught me
in the sixth grade,
with a full-body's sense
of space, meaning?

My eyes disparage distance,
or at least they don't think
in terms of miles. I'm happy
with the rush, the sprinter's gift
of sucking air and returning
fumes ten-fold, lungs burning.

Now and again, my stride cracks,
my gait slowing to an awkward swing,
hobbling, trying to find my balance
'cause suddenly I'm in a familiar field,
one that hurt, or at least seems the same,
except there are fire hydrants
where the bluestem should be.

Or reading D. Nurkse, I'm driven
to a dead halt, coughing, fighting
for room in my chest after seeing

how I felt when [that thing happened]
played out on Pearl Street. I close
the book, can't move, and all I can think
is two loud things: One, I am sick
of reading poems about Brooklyn. Two,
I can't imagine a place more beautiful.

DRINKS WITH OLD FRIENDS

Somewhere along the way,
the laughter changes timbre.
Judgmental highs
where the playful goads used to be —
the jabs you were all comfortable with —
and not only are they mocking you,
but you're doing it yourself.
Living for the night as your best critic:
a bald-spot, a leather chair, and an audience.
A bar tab a mile long.

Eight o'clock is going to feel great.

THE LOOK YOU GET WHEN YOU'RE LATE FOR FOR WORK BECAUSE YOUR THERAPY SESSION WENT OVER TIME

Beginning with you, let's reinvent the wheel, how you got here in the first place. How you launched up out of your hole, finally showered and are kinda looking good for once. It's not enough. There's a book, a method for critical engagement that you can't really buy, not at any store in this town. It's better to have already read it, to have somehow been born with the manual etched in the walls of your lungs, so whenever you speak, it lands just right. Sounds like you buy your polo shirts with gold bars and have never been late for a meeting.

AT THE BACK OF THE ROOM

To dance here is a long pour,
a steady game of sway and nod.
Shoes pump lazily, cool.
Get the shoulders to guide the hips
without the tell-tale jerk of a grooveless newbie.
I'm the spastic outsider,
wearing a glaring pose
against a crowd's celebrity lean.
The polish of style and musical bones.

I want to jump in.
Stand in the same gentle wake
and feel the pulsing warmth
in the toes of my (wrong) sneakers.
I imagine it's rocket fuel,
the kind of heat that shakes you
then sends you soaring,
but realistically, it wouldn't stick to me.
Like an electric blanket,
it would spark too quick
and fall too short
in a blaze of fake and unstable
glory. I wish.

VACATION
For Tyler

We're back at the hotel, on the very edge of Lincoln, awash with all the feelings a proper vacation can christen you with. Craft beer downtown, the basement smell of the arcade bar, the awkward, but electrifying run-ins with the concert-goers we kept bumping into. Then another couple rounds before we called it a night.

We only smoke when we're away from home and I guess it felt right, because we stopped for cigarettes and cheetos, and yes, more beer and we're all relatively speechless, taking long drags in the parking lot, drawing circles in the night with our cherries, propping up some poor light pole with our backs.

Even when Orlando calls you by a different name, even when the mood is shattered by the onslaught of juvenile *remember whens* and the goaty chug of drunken laughter, we still feel pretty damn cool, pretty certain that Lincoln is the best time we've ever had.

NOSTALGIA

Tried to recreate the last supper.
A lot of hugs and future plans,
places we'd meet. Places
we'd come back to, order the usual.

I order it all of the time,
at the head of the table,
though I'm the only one eating,
the only one here.

It's close. The same soundtrack,
but warped from the heat,
making everything sound thinner,
distant, with a thin coat of static.

I can almost grab it,
just beyond the seams
of my hoodie pockets.
In the next post on my newsfeed,
or the one after that.

I pay for this, too.
Hard-earned money, longer hours,
just for standing room in the mezzanine
of my own memories. Maybe,
if I called my girlfriend nostalgia
I'd go home more often.

LISTENING TO SKIP JAMES

My only memories of Mississippi are a Biloxi motel
and a spot of woods in Hattiesburg
where a woman I call freckles
undressed in front if me
for the third time.

But I've been crying
to the Bentonia school
since I was fifteen, learning new names
to call the devil.

Why is heartache always the woman's fault?
I didn't ask. Not until it was too late,
not until I had squandered my high school years
filling composition notebooks
with the top ten things I hate about myself.
Or was it the top ten reasons I was alone?

Projecting has always come naturally.

VIKING

Okay, so starting now...

I say as I hope
my calendar holds a linear
version of salvation.

Monday
will mark the beginning:

a brand new shore to beach my
viking ship upon.

And then I pretend
that I'll do anything but burn the huts
and relish in the destruction.

An *X* for every day I didn't

drink four pitchers,
or eat my weight in onion rings.
For every night spent alone
without shout-crying at the carpet.

SIX SHOOTER BLUES

Abe Lincoln just came back and started taking selfies.
Meanwhile, the hipster army turned
every bar into a museum with names
like *Where are all the honest men?*

Witches were flying matchsticks
'round the minimum wage,
daily pay crowd, flaunting
faces like goblins and legs of steel.

The cowboys paid no mind
and were riding bigger horses
than before. Mud, women, flags
tobacco all flapped behind the tires.

Keyboards were playing flamenco,
citing record collections stolen
from my Dad, I think.
Probably the clothes, too.

The brewer never texted back,
but I guess death is an excuse.
Who knew his teeth would turn
Blue? He was cold enough to drink,

especially since jazz stopped
being music and became
a conversation -- asking
without questions, counting
without numbers.

All the walls were covered
with the same two pictures
(but with different autographs):
paintings of foreign lovers. Exoticization

of the other is only the latest
fad, but if food comes in cans
then why shouldn't life
be the same? Preservatives

for dinner, for adventure
stored on our pocket-worn televisions.
Who needs a watch? Tumor-building
geniuses made a fortune

while Phileas Fogg rolls
in his grave (currently
being trampled by who knows what).
The interstate killed the rodeo star

and now all the rugged men
lost their hitchhiker thumbs to sloth
and smoke ultra-lights
with conviction. Street cred

based on paper-cut astronauts
and multi-tasking plate jugglers.
Vaguely, I thought of Spanish women
and searched my neck for a place to hang

a leather vest. I wanted to be the one
to punch that bastard across a saloon floor,
but no one fights there without
putting their findings in a newsletter.

They Fail because of instead of attacking the problem in which the character is caught, they lament it.

"Writing the Broadway Musical" - Aaron Frankel

None of this is important, but all of it is...

"The Last True Love Story" - Brendan Keiley

HIPSTER

Nestled khaki god,
see what you have made,
brandished pieces notwithstanding.
A found-object life
shiny with woman's approval,
especially in the right light, at the right angle.
The world teeters when he speaks now,
parents bow when he walks now,
and his dick operates
on his artistic edge.

DEFIBRILLATOR

Just a patinated Kaliningrad, standing still for its master and hating the northern sea. Some exclave chamber of my heart, beating for no reason, its hallways going nowhere, doors flapping for just anyone. A flagpole if I ever saw one, daring to be high enough, hoping the banner spirals in the wind the right way. Remembering letters finished with little bland kisses, dried and flaking lipstick stains the color of boiled hot dogs. Scented paper. Waking some plumbing I didn't know still existed.

BOMBAY

Sparkling stemware
cleaned and dried with hundred dollar bills
by men too young to own bow ties,
but here they are
sporting machine-sewn knots,
reeking of machine-cut forests.
I try to sniff the line
where juniper begins
and their after shave
(liberally applied, practically dripping
off chins much sharper than mine)
ends. It smells like arbor day.

My date invites their hands
to her suddenly soft shoulder
turned warm by tonic water.
Sapphire gin, baby blue eyes.
A whole row of pearls
flashing to be plucked and carried
when this wedding has ended
and the booze has found itself
as fuel. Fertilizer
to grow those wild oats.

I guess I'll take a cab home.

MOLEHILLS

I make friends
out of molehills

and have been seen scaling
cliffs far beyond my welcome.

From even the most casual encounters,
I have carried back souvenir flowers,

like those SS warriors who sought
edelweiss to prove they could do it

before they pissed vinegar and hate.
I do it for love

and only to have them snatched.
alienated hands or

the inevitable
interloper. Undeserving,

but the right place, the right shape
the right time.

Sentimental ropes
still hold me, lift me

up, up, up
and let me go, leave me

with a beautiful view
to cry from.

MEETCUTE

The gin-lipped lovers in swing and sweat
have been replaced
with the horn-rimmed smokers
that dirty the streets
and I don't want to be young anymore.
Where curbs would hold trophy
the reddened cheeks of kids too shy to kiss,
now, they wait for an Uber,
desperate for the gridlock,
equating and crashing until
licenses get removed, or drivers
grow out of fashion.

SPITTING

All the sapiosexual
twenty-somethings
in heat.

Mating rituals ensue:
made up in neon,
batting lashes,
though it's not needed.

The men are glowing,
musing at their enlightenment,
but still spitting like their fathers.

These are my peers? I asked
myself, the only one
okay with just being,
just drinking.

Conversation as contest:
bragging of taste,
spinning webs,

spinning at thirty-three
and a third
RPMs and blaring the trademark beat
of ownership.

Cheap beer, but the right moves
swivel, sniff, and sample.
Better than I remember.

Targets acquired
through a thistle glass scope
to lay waste to what could've been
a delightful evening.

What about you?
and the argument sloshes, splashing
chlorine in everyone's eyes, mouths.

I'm struggling to care,
so I swallow
my entire foot, and grab
one for the road.

THANKSGIVING BREAK AT THE BRASS RAIL
For Orlando Garcia

My white shirt fit so well, I didn't even wear anything over it. Yeah, it was winter, but what is the cold against brand new confidence, still in its plastic wrap.

The bar was practically empty and I had you laughing, saying *you lucky bastard* within minutes.

It was thanksgiving break. I was 15 pounds lighter, freshly single, and stranded, at least as far as family was concerned.

But who says family can't be borne out of whatever it's called when your life strips you of everything? Then one day, it's all the way into late afternoon, you wake up, you pull an old white undershirt from the back seat of your car and it fits so well. And on that day, the crack of a wishbone sounds just like two glasses clinking to your new found freedom.

IN MY MEMORY, THINGS ALWAYS HAPPEN IN WINTER
For Taylor Deutscher

Dreams aren't winter coats,
reminders of seasons that fit better,
woolen dust sponges we leave to die in a closet
and replace long before we need to.

And you can hide behind them all you want,
but I still see you, in the shadows,
all your talent spilling around the edges.

And I remember exactly what you looked like:
confidence,
resolute and red against the wind's bitter bite,
the cold that couldn't tame you,
couldn't keep you indoors.

That coat is still there,
hanging, dusty but ready
for an excuse to look good again,
a warm and sturdy purpose.

THE WAR THE NIGHT BEFORE

The choir lifts and falls with the shame of a Saturday. Rising gray and hinge-be-used…
abused is more like it. The backfire scares the neighbors. Next time. I'll talk to them tomorrow.
Meanwhile, with Hector long dead, the front yard tobacco catapults fire and retreat in a simultaneous and insincere gesture of selfish thought.

Shadows become dignitaries. The lilt of good-time myths reaches daggers into friendly backs.
It won't hurt until the morning. Boulder-tongued and careless, we seem to dig ditches and canals and gulfs between us and the nearest handshake. Without the savior tug of a yellow-cast shoulder, we drown and fight for a flex and silicon body to warm our hands in his plastic and button-whore gown.

The veteran sonofabitch, we've all come to be without leaves late and falls early. We hate him because he knows. We hate him because he could have stopped us. We hate him because he is too cool to suffer. At least, he does it on his own. We hate him because he finishes without us, in a smaller and colder hole with sentimental wax and electrolytes. We hate him because he wakes without the dull buzz of car-crashed neurons and the heated pins of familiarity. We hate him because we didn't listen.

MICHIGAN GOODBYE

And on his way out the door, he stopped to say something incredibly insightful, but it wasn't heard so he had to repeat it, and then a phone went off with the pre-recorded wails of a fire truck. Then, an espresso maker blew its two cents into a cup of soy milk and someone sneezed and we all started to feel how loud it was, how uncomfortable our chairs were, how we wished he just left and we didn't have to live in this moment any longer. But he waited. He waited for what felt like hours for a lull, living the horror of making a bed by oneself, one rebellious flap of the sheet always refusing to marry its betrothed corner. But finally a calm settled on the room and he muttered, *have fun without me.* We did.

OVERTHINKING

I actually love Magritte so much,
I've found myself browsing Amazon,
pricing bowler hats, preparing
justifications: *Oh this old thing?"
"It was a gag gift —
funny, right?* Anything other than
I thought it was cool, thought
it would make me a tad more interesting.

But I won't do it, 'cause I don't want to wear
the coolest hat,
for innocent self-esteem reasons,
and get mistaken
for the coffee-shop, soul-patch dragons,
the beasts breathing *friend-zone*
in non-filtered plumes of smoke.

But somewhere,
trying and not trying become
two heads of the same whatever,
a double-bladed cliché that
makes you feel like you're wearing
a dumb hat and everyone's pointing,
especially when you hear it
from one of those *friend-zone* guys.

UPON DISCOVERING THE INTERROBANG

I've long since mastered the art
of feigning surprise. My pen gasps,
shouts in the same tired way as everyone else's.

But once, someone had the nerve
to dream, to form beauty out of the aether,
to leave our curveless hearts to stand in shock.

I've written plenty,
but I've never had that courage,
or such a talent for naming things.

APOLOGIES

And then, just like any other grand gesture,
it bounced off of pre-war woodwork,
off of chandeliers so high,
even the cobwebs seemed to be made of fluted gold,
off of gleaming teeth
and landed with a dull thud,
a near-silent reminder
that theatrics are only needed
in place of the real thing,
that if you're hanging so many lights,
it's probably because you're scared of your own shadow,
or the way you really are in the dark,
just a quivering mess,
a pile of letters so desperate
even the mailman leaves you on read,
and meanders on to the next home.

GEORGIA

Two, oozy red beers deep
and heaven's guide-on greets me again,
brings me chili fries and a playful purse of the lips.
I am not an idiot and I'm not even shopping,
but tell that to my pen
'cause I'm writing an opera on my ticket,
a love song for four voices
and a chorale composed entirely in numerals,
a big enough tip to pay for her tuition.

MAYBE WE SHOULD TALK ABOUT THE BACHANTES ALWAYS BEING THE BUTT OF A JOKE WHEN REALLY THEY WERE JUST LIVING THEIR BEST LIVES

I've done some dumb things
in the name of wine:
sweating or crying,
in bed or on the floor,
in company or alone.

I've never brought God
into it, but if I had,
I'm sure I would have been there, too,

panting under that tree,
Pentheus' bloody hand in my hand,
hollering into the night,
over everyone else's hollers,
something akin to a prayer.

Dionysus, don't save me, not from this.
The world burns crueler in the morning,
and as I lay me down to purge,
know this is exactly how I thought this night would end,
and it didn't stop me. I am unstoppable. I am unstoppable.

THE BOSS IS IN A MOOD AGAIN

You are more than this spreadsheet, more than this nine am meeting you're dreading, more than her voice, more than a data specialist and her catechist scissor hands, cutting up your life story, writing it on the back of a distribution plan and sharing it with her neighbor, you are more than distribution plans, more than the brownies you didn't even want, but will take in spite of the diet you told everyone about, but they all dismiss *oh honey, you're not fat, doctors never know what they're talking about,* you are more than their confidence, their ability to pull the chair from under a medical professional just because they like the taste of chocolate, you are more than your inbox, no body, physical or galactic has held more than you, not even your unread, unlistened-to messages reminding you that you still haven't looked at the next meeting's agenda, you are more than the lie you tell, *yeah, the agenda looks great, nothing to add, nothing ever,* you are more than business cards, no one's life has such sharp edges, you are more than this office, you are more than the pictures you keep knocking over because the cord of the poorly placed telephone is also more than your pictures, you are more than your paystub, than printer ink, you are more than the dinner auction where you pretend to bid on things, knowing the implement dealer on the other side of the room will get the season tickets, you are more than the real reason you came, the open bar, because you had to, because if you didn't will you join the growing list of cursed names that drip as shadows from the water cooler, you are more

than buzzed coworkers mocking specially curled
or straightened hair for this night of elbow rubbing, than
this conference, because when the sun comes back to
Overland Park in the morning, you get to check out of
your hotel and leave, more than this nagging feeling that
you're lazy because we both know if it were up to you
you'd spend every waking minute doing something that
mattered, something that didn't grate your skin cells and
energy through your keyboard they still haven't replaced,
even though it stops working twice a day, something
bigger than monthly staff meetings, something
profoundly steady and wet with purpose, something
more than inside jokes about coworkers who walked the
plank so long ago, more than a thousand of us.

Passion's a precipice –
so won't you please
move away?
Move away,
please!

"Attitude to a Miss" - Vladmir Mayakovsky

Human beings...seldom deny themselves the pleasure of exercising a power which they are conscious of possessing, even though that power consist only in a capacity to make others wretched.

"The Professor" - Charlotte Brontë

DIRT DOG

don't worry about him, he's a dirt road expressionist,
writes love songs about motorcycles, gets in fistfights,
usually because his words are as greasy as he pretends his
hands get, don't listen, he'll calm down when he feels like
no one is looking, he has a habit of stealing pens from
waitresses, working on his masterpiece, five stanzas on
the feeling of wind as it blows passed his uncaged heart,
about liberty in the Townshend sense, in the no seat belt,
no one tells me how to put one shoe on before the other
sense, in the crushed cans all over his living room floor
and incense sense, no, he means what he manages to say
out loud, but let it roll off your shoulders, because his
spine trembles under all that leather and barking at the
mailman is all he's got

ACHILLES

I saw Achilles in Lafayette Park.
His helmet, a soppy mess of smeared ink,
was catching the rain as he hid,
and sporting headlines of his own making.
He kept his heel in a brown paper bag,
kissing it often and feeling stronger for it.
Meanwhile,
the king pressed on.
Separated by yards,
but connected by history.

EVERYDAY

You never just share your everyday
thoughts about breakfast, about eggs,
perfect, peppered and stacked on wheat toast,
or about the song you heard, had your head
swaying, or the dog you saw on your way in,
to work, to school, or wherever you go
when you're not here, proving yourself.

Your everyday is always propped
against Armageddon. You speak in slow
waiters and war stories, idiots, and *oh,
I've gotten really good at putting
[them] in their place.* But you have to,
of course, of course. You're attacked
for walking outside, for expecting
the very least from everyone you meet.

I've seen a lot, but I've never seen soup
sent back quite so many times. Now,
you've never worked a real job,
but I can only believe you, you'd do it
so much better. You're such a good driver,
too, able to take up so many lanes.
We still feel for your poverty
of spirit, of scapegoats, of courage
to face mirrors directly.
You must really suffer
from suffering just like us.

THE SOCIAL CONTRACT

I'm flying
into San Francisco, my coffee
now the Exxon Valdez,
its crude killing the light,
coating my tablet, my ebook closed
while I wait, the attendant sprinting with napkins.

And I ask myself,

because we are all philosophers
at thirty-four thousand feet, as we sit
throned above almost everyone else:

Would it just knock Rousseau out to know
that I read,
One thinks himself the master of others and still remains
a greater slave than they,
and that it lit the same wick
it always does, even after a hundred
times through this very subject?

Would he blush or swell
with pride at the city buses keeping
this idea moving in my head, dropping me
off at every municipal building,
to wreak democracy the right way:
laying pipe, running cable,
cleaning oil spills?

Would it just knock him out to know
that I didn't even read
the three privacy policies
I blindly clicked through
to power on the device for the first time,
get the app to get his book
in the first place?

SMARTER AFTER MIDNIGHT

Quite the two-dollar-you-call-it sophist,
I can often be found down among the dead men,
eyes half-surrendered, floating.

Quoting W.C. Fields, defending Rupi Kaur
from the liberal arts army gathered and chanting
lines from my diploma,
claiming that one cancels out the other.

They break out in some perspicuous mode
of dance as they sing, not of love, but orthology.

Of lyrics so dense, one must travel
with a ProQuest subscription
in order to weep at their beauty.

I just like to love things.

WHEEL OF FORTUNE

The early pains of evening. America sat to be charmed by his handsome suit, her Hollywood dress, bringing language to light in the aquarium walls.

A turn of the lurid spokes, aglitter with pocket money and summer homes well deserved. A common phrase, a place, a thing, the canned good-time wishes of an audience eager to please, dying to stand in that place.

Commercial breaks become so duh, so well yeah, if I had that kind of money, of course I'd buy a new Hyundai, of course, I'd outfit my kids in the K-Mart summer spectacular. They can leave their shirts to hang from their back pockets as they lounge on our speedboat, catching a kind of wind that has always existed, but could never afford until now, now that the little eyelash stopped ticking against the rods and the wheel stops and it gives, it gives, it gives, or it takes, it takes away.

I FOUND LOVE ON THE BLOCKCHAIN

I found love on the blockchain
and had the sense
to buy a ring,
but I didn't know I was kneeling
in gravel.
A little, encrypted groan
let out and was lost to the sounds,
the footsteps of Buckingham guards
spinning passwords like toy rifles.
They had the nerve
to ask my mother's maiden name,
my favorite restaurant in college, whatever
out-of-town review boards require these days.

I found love on the blockchain
and gave myself away.
I danced and took envelopes
full of drops from bandwidth junkies
who are still cruising apps
for nickels.
I am leaping into bed
with the gray men, bounding
one shiny gate at a time.
Making a future, sure,
but leaving trails accordingly,
thinking I'm a clever guy.

Diamonds cut glass,
and everything else we see through, apparently,
so, I take it, learn to love it
kiss the lips, the rings of royalty and rest
my head on a regal lap.
Whatever ATMs require these days.

I found love on the blockchain,
but prenups now withholding,
I am lost to the cost of things.
Whatever love requires these days.

FIRST STEADY PAYCHECK AND HE'S TROLLING

He's careful to adjust the bass before
turning onto Barclay Drive.
The ladies tend their gardens, gawk
at their neighbors' lawns and make hay
out of noticing him.

These aren't the mansions
on the west side, but here
the houses stand alone,
porches heating, fences making
summer a private affair.

Kids clear the street,
to let the gray Impala
pass as he plays music —
heavy on the chill,
but doesn't belong to him.

They're used to cars
one shade brighter, five years newer
as they slide inside three-car garages
to be protected
from the elements, appreciation.

Parents shake their head as if
that wasn't his intention
and eventually, he goes back home,
back to work, his own neighborhood.
He parks his car in the street.

Of course, he doesn't have a choice,
but he didn't get a loan
to keep his car a secret,
to keep his speakers quiet,
to keep it parked too long.

IT'S A FREQUENCY THING

I hear the call.
In a two-trumpet swoon,
or a clarinet honking
it's agreement, I hear it.

It's in sweaty
pierogi guts and garlic breath,
hairy men and pursed lips.
Papal gestures imported
via diocesan rags.

Bond villains and the wrenched
victims of older wars
puffs Poland in my ear,
glued to every radio with reach.

Language books,
though restful, sing
anthem and praise
in the same cracked pitch that I do.

Ellis Island tales are for other people,
but I can still smell the sea.
And I can fit everything
I care about in a single suitcase.

DEAR SATOSHI

If you won't speak, let me speak
to you, behind as many screens as you'd like.

I keep my geography marked.
A map on my desktop, little red icons, those
people who were with me.
Memories made real by the tone
in their voice, on teamspeak as they said
we're here because the difference
between *finally* and *finally*
is unmanageable.

Travelling alone is fine
the way protein is protein
and that once you've eaten, it doesn't matter
what you were in the mood for, or
who paid the delivery guy.
But every meal tastes better
in company, appetites governed
by conversation,
savored bites in between.

But I'm hodling
my breath for the day that price and time
mean the same thing. For the day my fans
can rest, hard drives, old smart phones cooling
in the shade of *we made it*.

Finally and to have that *finally*
wake me in the night, 'cause its arrival
will ring louder than any trumpet,
than any vibrating thing ever has before.

ELEGY FOR INDUSTRY

The city air is cleaner now,
but they hate the smell.
It is hollow like a song
sung without meaning.
Their nostrils
long for the harsher, quilled
haze of industrial fumes
that speak: *the city lives
and has the body odor,
the factory breath to prove it.*
Clean air is sweet,
too sweet, repulsive
to the workers at home,
pretending there is not a problem,
as if the kids haven't figured it out
on their own.

The streets are empty of purpose,
but filled with stoop smokers,
children long since tired
of their stomping grounds.
Playing is habit,
as is longingly looking
at the sky, suddenly bright
and pumping with color,

animals, clouds
(the non-artificial sort),
and the occasional dusty trail
of a plane that would never dare steer close
to this city of all cities.

They'd cheer for their children's lungs
if they weren't so scared
for their bellies,
for the new and far latitude
where the sky still swallows black
while a different set of hands
draws, pours,
feels
the oil and works the curves
of the machines
the city weeps for.

THESIS

My thesis was bound, came like a bad breakup:
all of a sudden and after too much work,

too many nights sweating, performing
surgery on the finest possible bits.

Insert a fallacy about investment,
months/years spent sinking cost,

sinking teeth into cold truths, shivering,
sinking in too deep to really breathe.

And the *finally* breath that I thought would lighten
my lungs, would let me rise back to the surface

of everyday stuff, the friends
I used to have time for,

just felt like I was punched in the chest:
Here you are. You are done now.

Now, I see her wherever I go.
Students sitting in a coffee shop.

Couples poring over books, so glossy,
so awake with some idea of a future.

Now I see her marbled spine everywhere, gold letters saying something about interest rates:

We will have your ass one day.

HERITAGE: KOBIETY

I don't know the women,
but I picture them strong.
Their names are echoes
of patron saints,
or famous travelers;
the heroines of cabbage eating people.
The men, though:
Vladislav, Vostok,
Wachek.

They saw men
on wood and linoleum stages.
They saw themselves
pulled by an aluminum bridle.
Men need nourishment,
even before the sun can shake its disapproval.
Electric veins course until lunch time.
Refill! Beer run!
Whiskey
under the gut and ready to burn
at a moment's notice.

Time cards:
the analog tick of sore bodies
and shameful performance.
Refill! Set them free!

Off to feel the gentle ease
of tension being replaced
with expectation.
Which echo will they hear after dinner?
Home,
or the nymph?

Musical interludes
of sweat and fun abroad
delay the inevitable.
The day isn't over
until vibrato folds to chemistry,
wife and babe feel the result,
and grow the bruises to prove it.

The drive —
we'll call it work ethic —
to do it all again,
in spite of sorrow and having anything better to do,
is something to be admired
in a cutesie, but dark denial-laden fashion.
So,
I guess I'm doing okay

I AM YOUNG

I write with a computer.
Longhand is a short game
and I am not a player.
My hands cramp too quickly
and my attention span is
philosophy, is it dead yet?
'Cause I read Barthes
the other day, but I'm sure
he'd say to go to bed
and stop looking for heroes
in my habits.
As long as he doesn't know
that I sleep with the TV on.

COMSUBLANT

Name a boat for me,
or for the amount of time I spent staring
into classroom ceiling tile,
dreaming of impact, beards, and height.
The commander I would have made
if only my joints enjoyed
the same cinema that I did.

If bravery rang from the calliope steam,
I would hold the cake;
a chutzpah market cornered
by resourceful hands
that crumble in the real world.
The spirit is lush,
but the flesh is bleak
like a Midwestern winter.
Ashy bark, limbs broken
under a delicate kiss of snow.

Scuttling requires a captain strong enough
to succumb to salt-water lungs,
crushing depths, and crass enough
to coax his crew to a place of self-preservation;
that part of them that should have never enlisted in the first place.
We hang mutineers because they remind us
that ropes come cheap,

but brass is forged
on anvils in a distant admiral's office
off the flames of sonorous sound bites.

They'll say I didn't try,
that my torpedoes were just stones
tossed by a kid to dance
along the faucet pond
in our collective backyards
and that all I did was talk shit.

THE NIGHT EDDY GOT REAL EXCITED

Because I slap motherfuckers, because the Gretch is a street built just for me, because I'll park in any direction that suits me, because I can lift my own body weight and look good doing it, my forehead a creaseless ode to the gods who sculpted me, I am marble, I am permanent and I am ready for all that permanency entails, because I don't have hangovers, or at least don't understand what one is, because when I tell people this, over their groans and churning stomachs, they look at me like I am invincible, or stupid, or maybe you can't be one without the other, because I may not know what a metaphor is, but my brazen behavior is a gold mine, a factory for figures of speech, proof of archetypal destinies, because I can play the guitar, even if it's just well enough to drown out the radio, because my Mustang is better than his Mustang, even with the ripped interior, even though my Mom bought it for me, even though I've never taken it over eighty-five, even though it wasn't enough to keep my girlfriend around, to keep her interested, because it will be enough to carry me anywhere I want to go, mountaintops and deserts, empty lots and stranded plains, enough room for me to stretch out, stare at the stars and ask 'How does the moon change shapes?' because I might have slept through science class, but I am suddenly good at making friends and fear I might have to return again, to the rising ford that knows no confidence, that only lets me stand as a sliver of the man I am right now.

everything is wild here
heavy rain & children
who grow like weeds

"The Way of Dandelions" - John Dorsey

Getting back there and finding out if it's as beautiful as I remember.

"Annie on my Mind" - Nancy Garden

WRITERS ARE GODS HERE

There are coffee shops in Kansas
and bookstores, too.
In little town libraries,
we heft real books
and dog-ear famous pages
as they do in other time zones.
Pretentious pricks quote Pynchon
with east-coast ease
and chests puffed on something
we don't even grow here,
but are fed in streamed doles
because their magazines won't ship
to our doorsteps.
Writers are gods here,
as long as their zip codes read
like a language we recognize,
but don't actually understand.
The homegrown, the sunflower sages
are perpetually, permanently
canonized wannabes
that prefer these cold, Midwestern shoulders
to New York deities
who never hear our prayers,
never even say thank you.

THE WORLD'S LONELIEST MOSHPIT, CIRCA 2004

When parking lots act like mountaintops, a chance to tower. Feeling higher than the rest of town, an expedition forming, a sound check filling the air with the rakey, thin voice of a scene kid playing a telecaster. A journey is defined by the quiver in your gut, not the destination, not the fact you'll be inside for the next three hours.

Inching closer to fellow humans, outside, waiting for the show to start. Kids in hoodies, chain smoking, wearing cargo shorts in January. Courage building its addictive foam at the corners of mouths, in the balls of feet, but will likely fade there. Will tonight be the night? Will I ride the breakdown, two-step as the bassist twirls his beast around his neck; *oh-so-hardcore* acrobatics? I'm more of an observer. My hood is up, though. And I think she is noticing ME this time.

PRESCRIBED BURNS

Fires are just the ground's way of saying what crops couldn't.
Something about how nothing really burns,
it just becomes a mix of ash and smoke, hangs
like greyscale Christmas lights on barbed wire fences
until a good gust of wind comes along, restores order,
and it all settles on gravel roads, or the toy-like
side panels of someone's Sunday cruiser.
They just don't make cars like they used to.

STILL

You're visiting and so you see
the friend who is left, still
in the tired town
you run from, still
wearing the same blue
corporate logo smock, still
here.

You look great, man,
he says, he climbs in and you make
familiar circles — the teenager
routes of main street, country roads,
and the parking lot where you fell
in love and into the wrong crowds. Still,

there are people,
new kids drinking
in pickup beds and swapping
keys and stories (lies) to get them
closer to adulthood.

You watch, shake your head,
remembering how dumb
you were.
He sighs, still
wishing he were one of them.

Beer is in order
and your old bar hasn't updated
since W., but the faces are older,
tired, looking at you.

You look like shit, you don't say.
You nod at his (non) stories
and pay the tab, still
guilty for ever leaving, and always
waiting to get the hell out of there.

ALL BEFORE YOU ENDED UP ON MY PORCH
For Daphne

It's your drumset, maybe,
or the way you talk about it.
The way you laugh above things,
as if you've already lived
through any joke I can muster.

Your pale, but warm skin
dressed in black
and ablaze with so many rosy feelings
we can't even begin to discuss,
not now, not in between our turns
on stage. It's play practice afterall,
rehearsing these parts we pretend to understand.

I'm better onstage, we both agree,
but it's back to the seats
to talk about everyone else,
whisper about the future,
to soak in your taste
in music, movies, anything.
And I'm just hoping
to catch some kind of blessing,
(we'll call it grace) and I find
myself waiting for it, everyday
I find myself willing
to do whatever Davey Havok tells me to.

HAVE YOU EVER SEEN A SUNSET

I don't mind saying that there are no sunsets
like Kansas sunsets, so much open space,
flat ground to fall to,
all knees and dropped jaws
at the pink, red slit in the sky.
Last time I was in New York,
a woman asked me if I had ever had a bagel
before and I wish we had that kind of arrogance.
That we were members of an elite
breakfast pastry society,
the only ones to have ever tasted
the things we hold dear.
And maybe arrogance isn't the right word.
She was probably trying to be nice, offering
a small slice of what brings her to the ground,
so from now on, whenever I make introductions,
I'll just ask *have you ever seen a sunset?*

HOME

We couldn't help but jump, the speakers rattling something shitty against the noise of the dirt road, but we knew this song like we knew our families, like we knew each other, the only four people in the world with good taste in music, who understand what a refuge you can find circling your hometown, like we knew these roads, worn grains in the cracked Midwestern wood, soft to the touch, but look like a splintered mess. We couldn't help but jump, thrashing our bodies to the bassline, *la-la-la-ing along, la-la-la-ing* like we knew what it was to be older, to be us in ten years, to be us still together, 'cause surely that's the way that works.

OUR MOTHERS AND THE MEN THAT GUIDE THEM

The younger men
of my neck of the woods,
gather at their rain-trodden stomping grounds.
They navigate battleship trucks
through the mud
until one is proven
to be better than the rest (commander).
The women gather there,
As they haven't missed this show
since the resurrection.

The boys, like roosters
pin calls of prowess
and *until morning,*
allowing lips to meet, separate,
sign terms, and promise rewards:
a fifty-five inch piece of glass.
It will mark where she belongs.
She will tell her neighbors
that it was what she wanted.

When the door is closed,
the curtains drawn,
the TV tells a different story.
Lips meet the lips of strangers,
deals are broken.

She wants to be one of the liars,
smokers, sexual beings
craving pain in her joints,
and tired brows, strained teeth.

Her mind wanders to a softer mattress
As foreign hands
quicken a pulse thought dead…
but…the deal she made
so many years before.

Leave the bending hips and smacking lips
to those who can bare to lose them.
I will take it straight. I will take it on my back.

BAPTISM

We threw our dumb blue hats
in the air, 'cause ritual is the difference
between childhood and now.

We disbursed, to embrace
our grandparents, and some
shiny responsibility. Walking back
to our families' cars as adults.

Then she found me to say,
Hey, good luck, man.

I remember the gown's Halloween
plastic feel and the subtle, but sad
way her lips leaned back
before she said
See you later.

Might have been the only time she spoke
to me since the sixth grade.
But it wasn't goodbye,

it was a baptism.
A cleansing wave,
erasing everything she had ever said

about me since the sixth grade.
Oh, but I took it. I smiled back
and a redeeming light
carried her home.

And she truly was forgiven.
The only one that said goodbye to me.
Mine or not, I kept that offering,

used it to buy a plaque:
People can surprise you.
I look at it
every time I think of high school.

People can surprise you. I mean,
I've lost track of how many people I've lost track of.

I often shuffle my thumb
to avoid messages from long-lost
hallway partners,
those people who locked eyes,
had something to say, but couldn't keep
such company in such a crowded place.

Locked eyes, but moved on and suddenly,
they find Jesus in their thirties,
and want me to drag them
into the Jordan,

'cause it's my job to hear confession,
to tap on the big man's shoulder:
You can let them in now.
Surely, they didn't mean it.

People can surprise you, I mean,
she didn't even accept my friendship
request on Facebook.

MAKEOUT SPOT

Always after dark, of course,
we would park by the municipal airport,
because you said it was remote.
But all corners in our town
were small, tidy, out of the way corners,
because we lived in the middle
of an historic nowhere. But really
I think it's something else.

It was the strange lights
along the runway, etching
their harsh red-orange say into
the tarmac, because love, especially fresh,
still-smells-and-crashes-like-the-sea love
is always that audacious, making
everything else seem blacker,
two breaths away
from taking the hell off into the stars.

RUST

I appreciate the rust.
[This thing] was here before me
and has the iron to prove it.
Brittle it may be,
but I was brittle once.
Found a way to fatten
my limbs, to bring them color,
to not flake away like
breaking leaves in fall,
or fish food between giving fingers.
I will not crumble. I will grease
the joints, but just enough
to bring utility full circle.
Always preserve the red,
orange, brown, and ugly sight.

GREEN

The kind of green that hurts my eyes:
pale and useless against the dark.
The seats were slick with summer's graces.

Hot
and jumping —
we couldn't help but jump —
we traded breath for music.

Sing,
soprano cast in green.
I'll hold the wheel and wait,
lending pause to thought
and thought to hurricane,
while hoping that the interlude allows
for a fly-by.

An unconfirmed sighting:
a sweet, if not imagined
brush of fingers, dumb in the dark
and a strand of hair (also lost to the music)
that looked absolutely perfect in green.
I got the whole thing on tape.

BIRTHDAY

Needing specific late night sustenance, we drove twenty miles for the neon promise of *open*. The same woman as last time: *finally, customers.* Took our order and made good on our extra cheese, jalapeno pizza with energy drinks, legal cigarettes, heartburn. Shared with the kind of friends they just don't make anymore. A midnight kiss from Josie.

In a rural gas station,
I turned eighteen.
I wish I was still there.

PRETTY AND NICE

She was the ultimate example
of a woman who is pretty and nice
to you — which never happens —
and so you think you're in love, suddenly
dropping dead birds at her feet and she's like
What the hell are you doing?
And you try to pretend
you're fluent in human, as if
all relationships aren't burdensome
messes, just chances to flex your
what-the-hell-are-you-doing muscles.

WHY DO YOU ACT LIKE THAT?

It's stupid how much all of this matters now.
Years since I hunched, pubescent and afraid of everything,
howling just to hear my voice echo back.
The comfort of knowing the walls were still there
without having to remove my hands from my eyes.

Lunchrooms are what I think death will be like.
Cold, isolated, gathered for a slimy feast.
A smell that vaguely reminds you of something that once lived,
while angels float around the room,
holding hands and passing love letters,
basking in the royal rays of gossip, status.

I was always loud because at least
the seraphs would look at me
before they broke for the trash cans.

GRAMMY AWARDS

Do you wish I looked like them?

We're watching together,
but you're not technically in the room.
We are on the phone, our own TVs tuned in,
gasping in unison every time a name is called,
pretending it affects us somehow.

Then, the moment we've been waiting for.
Andre 3000 sings your favorite song,
and I can hear you smiling,
even through the gross display of cultural insensitivity
we don't yet understand
playing out before us. At first,
I'm loving it.
A whole stage of long legs
and we're both *this is so good,*
but then I can hear your smile fade.
My neck loses its rhythmic flex and you ask
if I wish you were something impossible.
Never.

I turn the TV off and we talk for hours.

Timothy Tarkelly's work has appeared in *Cauldron Anthology, Aphelion Webzine, Philosophical Idiot, Peculiars Magazine, Back Patio Press, Tiny Essays, Detritus Online,* and others. His book *Gently in Manner, Strongly in Deed: Poems on Eisenhower* was published by Spartan Press in April 2019. When he's not writing, he teaches in Southeast Kansas. You can find more of his work at www.timothy tarkelly.com

www.ingramcontent.com/pod-product-compliance
Lightning Source LLC
Chambersburg PA
CBHW022011120526
44592CB00034B/778